W9-BYG-296

BASEBALL

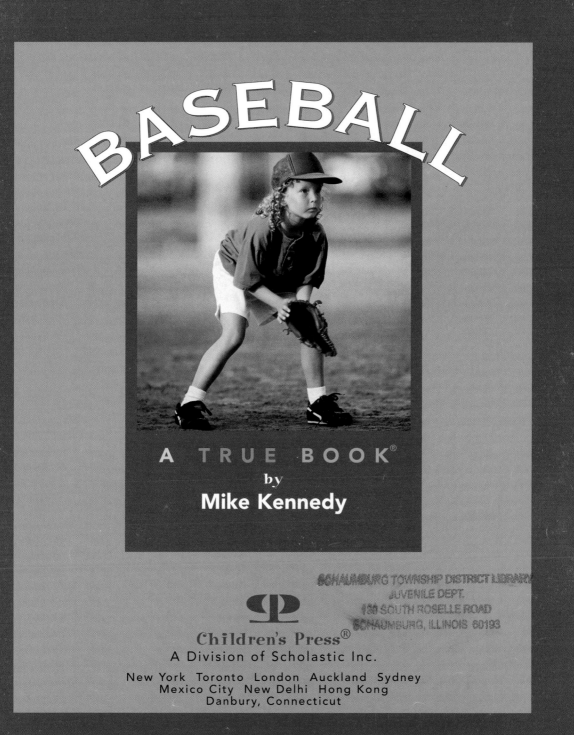

A TRUE BOOK®

by

Mike Kennedy

Children's Press®
A Division of Scholastic Inc.

New York Toronto London Auckland Sydney
Mexico City New Delhi Hong Kong
Danbury, Connecticut

796.357
KENNEDY, M
3 1257 01545 7913

**An umpire signaling
that a runner is safe**

Reading Consultant
Nanci R. Vargus, Ed.D.
Teacher in Residence
University of Indianapolis
Indianapolis, Indiana

The photograph on the cover
shows a Little League player
at bat. The photograph on
the title page shows a young
player waiting to field a ball.

Library of Congress Cataloging-in-Publication Data

Kennedy, Mike (Mike William), 1965-
    Baseball / by Mike Kennedy.
        p. cm.—(A True book)
    Summary: Presents the history, rules, equipment, and positions of
baseball, as well as a list of some of the best players of all time.
    Includes bibliographical references and index.
    ISBN 0-516-22334-8 (lib. bdg.)   0-516-29371-0 (pbk.)
    1. Baseball—Juvenile literature. [1. Baseball.] I. Title. II. Series.
GV867.5.K46 2002
796.357—dc21

2002005321

Contents

A batter awaiting the pitch

Covering the Bases

To understand the United States, you first have to understand baseball. A famous writer once wrote words similar to those. Maybe he was right. Baseball has been this country's "national **pastime**" for well over 100 years.

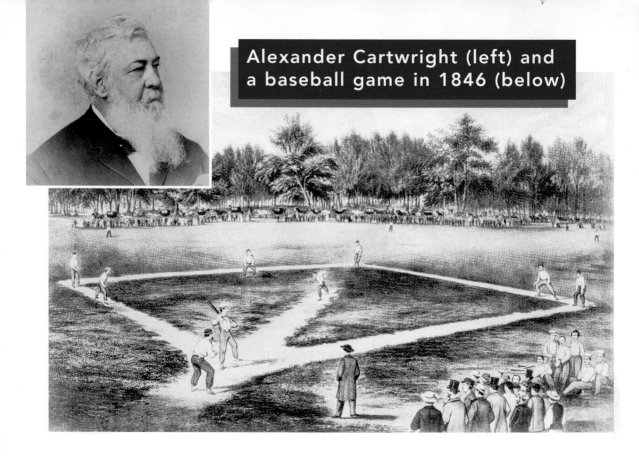

Alexander Cartwright (left) and a baseball game in 1846 (below)

Many people regard Alexander J. Cartwright as the "father" of baseball. In the 1840s, he organized the game's first real team: the Knickerbocker Base Ball Club.

Cartwright also introduced many of the rules used to this day. Within 20 years, hundreds of teams throughout the northern United States played baseball. When Northern soldiers were captured during the Civil War (1861–1865), they taught the sport to their Southern guards.

By the 1870s, baseball had become so competitive that teams paid their best players. In 1876, many of these **professionals** joined the National League (NL)

for its first season. The American
League (AL) set up shop 25
years later. In 1903, the rival
leagues sent their best teams to
the World Series. Today, the NL
and AL champs still meet in this
"Fall Classic" to determine
baseball's top team.

For a long time, the game was played much differently than it is now. Batters used square bats, and pitchers threw underhand. The ball was mushier, too. That meant fielders could play without gloves.

In the early days of baseball, fielders played barehanded.

Hitting a home run was almost impossible because the ball didn't spring off the bat like it does today. Baseball finally took its modern form in the 1890s.

The game still was not perfect. It wasn't until 1947 that people of all races were allowed to play in the major leagues. That is when baseball truly became America's national game.

Batter Up

When two teams square off in a baseball game, they **alternate** between offense and defense. The team at bat is on offense, and the team in the field is on defense. When the team on defense records three outs, they get a chance to hit. The team with the most runs at the end of the game is the winner.

The visiting team bats in the first half (or "top") of each inning, and the home team in the second half (or "bottom"). Professionals play nine innings. Little Leaguers play six. Tie games are decided in extra innings, which go until one team outscores the other.

The goal on offense is to score as many runs as possible before making three outs. A run is scored when a batter touches first, second, and third

This batter is about to make contact with the pitch (top left). A runner rounds second and heads for third (top right). Be sure to touch the plate when sliding into home (bottom right).

base, and then crosses home plate without being called out by an **umpire**.

Each batter tries to reach base safely. Players hit according to the batting order set by the **manager**.

Hitting a pitch is difficult. If you swing and miss, you are charged with a strike. A ball batted into foul territory is also a strike. Foul territory is the area outside the white lines running from home plate through first and third base into the outfield.

You can also get a strike if you don't swing at a pitch that the umpire decides has sailed

fair territory

foul territory

foul territory

foul territory

This photo shows fair territory and foul territory.

through the "strike zone." The strike zone is the area above home plate between the batter's knees and chest.

If you get three strikes, you are out. However, you cannot strike out on a foul ball. In

A swing
and a miss
is a strike.

other words, if you already
have two strikes, you can hit
an unlimited number of fouls.

When batting, keep both
eyes on the ball and swing the
bat smoothly. Run to first base
whenever you hit a pitch. A
ball popped in the air and
caught before it falls to the

ground is an out. It doesn't matter if the hit is fair or foul. The rules are different if a fair ball hits the ground. Here you can advance to first safely if you reach the base before the defense throws the ball there.

Another way to reach base is to "walk." A batter gets to go

A walk is a free pass to first base.

to first if the pitcher throws four "balls" before three strikes. A ball is any pitch not swung at by the hitter that does not pass through the strike zone.

Once on base, runners may advance to the next one at their own risk. You can take more than one base, but you can't move onto the one in front of you if a teammate is already on it. Only one runner is allowed on each base. If you wander off a base and a fielder tags you with the ball, you are out.

There are two ways to slide into a base: feet first (left) and head first (below).

If you hit the ball far enough, you just might circle the bases for a home run.

When a batter hits the ball fair, it's a good opportunity for the runners on base to advance. If a hit goes far enough, a runner might even advance all the way to home plate to score a run.

With less than two outs, a player on base shouldn't run too far on a ball hit in the air. If the team on defense catches it, you must return to the base you were on. The fielding team can record another out by throwing to the base you left before you return there.

Taking the Field

On defense, your goal is to stop the other team from scoring runs. Nine players in all work together to do this. Six are stationed in the infield and three in the outfield. The infield is the portion of the field that surrounds the bases and pitcher's mound. The

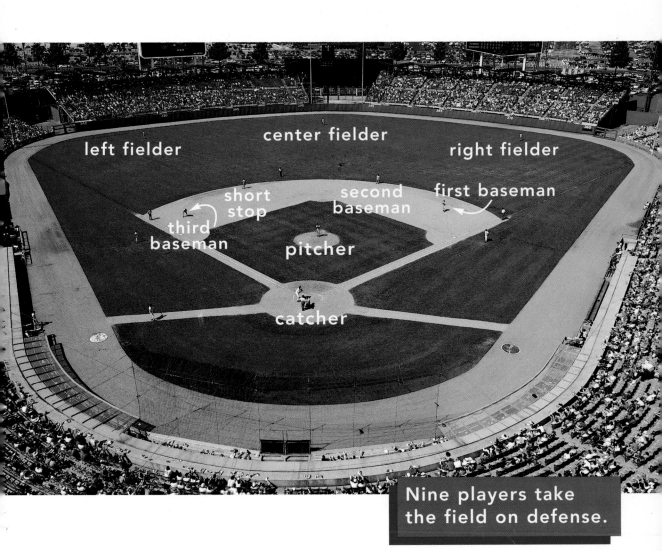

left fielder

center fielder

right fielder

short stop

second baseman

first baseman

third baseman

pitcher

catcher

Nine players take the field on defense.

outfield is all the territory that
extends beyond the infield.

To create power, a pitcher uses a "wind up" before throwing the pitch.

The pitcher starts the action by delivering the ball to home plate from the pitcher's mound.

A pitcher's job is to throw pitches that are hard for batters to hit or that the umpire calls for strikes. Pitchers need to be able to put the ball where they want it. This is called having good control. In other words, **precision** is just as important to pitching as speed.

The catcher, knowing the strengths and weaknesses of each batter, lets the pitcher know where to best aim the pitch within the strike zone.

The catcher squats behind home plate to receive pitches.

That is the "easy" part of catching. The hard part is crouching behind the plate for an entire game and blocking "wild" pitches thrown in the dirt. If a catcher misses a wild pitch, anyone on base has a chance to advance.

The first baseman and second baseman play on the right side of the infield. The third baseman and shortstop play on the left.

The top responsibility of these infielders is to stop ground balls hit in fair territory and then throw to first base for an out. This is called a force play.

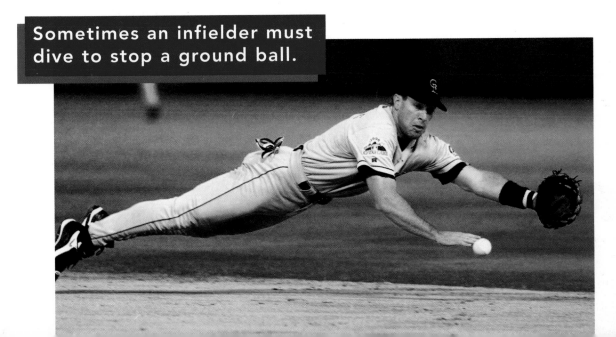

Sometimes an infielder must dive to stop a ground ball.

The defense can also force runners at other bases. For example, if the bases are "loaded" with runners, you can record force outs at second, third, and home, too.

The first baseman normally receives throws to first from the other infielders, including the pitcher and catcher. Around the rest of the infield, the second baseman and shortstop team up to cover the area around second base.

The fielder must keep his foot on the base when catching a throw for a force out.

Third base is called the "hot corner," because the ball gets there so fast. Third basemen need quick **reflexes** and a strong throwing arm.

What a catch! (left). Throws from the outfield should be hard and accurate (above).

Like infielders, outfielders can record an out by catching a ball hit in the air before it lands on the ground. But judging a ball's flight correctly from the outfield is more difficult because you are farther from home plate. When a "fly ball" is hit between two outfielders, one must "call" the ball while it is in the air to avoid a collision.

Right fielders need powerful arms, because they have to make the longest throws. Center fielders often range into left and right, so they usually have good speed. Left field is the easiest outfield position to play, though it can be the busiest, too.

Ten You Should Know

Who is the greatest player in baseball history? Here are ten of the best:

Ty Cobb

Ty Cobb, OF, 1905–1928
The Georgia Peach has baseball's highest lifetime batting average (.367).

Babe Ruth

Babe Ruth, OF & P, 1914–1935
After a few years as the game's top pitcher, the Bambino became the most feared hitter ever.

Josh Gibson

Josh Gibson, C, 1930–1946
Those who saw him in the Negro Leagues say he was the most powerful hitter ever.

Ted Williams

Ted Williams, OF, 1939–1942 and 1946–1960
The Splendid Splinter was tall and skinny and had the smoothest swing of all time.

Jackie Robinson, IF, 1947–1956

Jackie Robinson

He suffered terrible treatment as the first African-American in the majors, and still performed so well he made the Hall of Fame.

Hank Aaron, OF, 1954–1976

Hammerin' Hank is baseball's all-time home run champ, with 755.

Hank Aaron

Sandy Koufax, P, 1955–1966

Sandy Koufax

He had a great fastball, a wicked curve, and a chance to toss a no-hitter every time he pitched.

Nolan Ryan, P, 1966–1993

Nolan Ryan

The Ryan Express struck out the most batters in big-league history.

Mark McGwire, 1B, 1984–2001

Mark McGwire

Big Mac could knock the ball out of any stadium.

Sammy Sosa, OF, 1989–

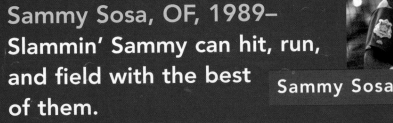

Sammy Sosa

Slammin' Sammy can hit, run, and field with the best of them.

Tools of the Trade

Baseball is also known as "hard-ball." Why? Because the ball is very hard. The yarn surrounding the rubber and cork center is wound tightly, and the cover is stitched snugly around that.

The bats used in baseball are made of wood or **aluminum**. Aluminum bats provide more

The stitching on a baseball is also known as the "seams" (above). A player should choose a bat that is easy to handle (right).

power. They are not allowed in professional or college baseball.

A bat should be easy to swing. Bigger is not always better. A player should try to make contact on the bat's "sweet spot." This section of the bat's **barrel** sends the ball the farthest.

For safety,
batters wear
padded helmets.

Players should always wear a batting helmet at the plate and while running the bases. It has plenty of padding to guard against head injuries.

You also need a glove or mitt to protect your hand when you field the ball. Every glove is designed with a "pocket" and webbing. This is the best area to catch the ball.

A first baseman's glove (above) is different than a catcher's mitt (right).

Some positions require special gloves. First basemen use long, oval gloves that are good for handling low throws. A catcher's glove is round and padded to soften the blow of fast pitches. Outfield and infield gloves are similar, though outfielders usually prefer a longer model.

Play Ball!

Every day during baseball
season, more than 5,000 people
show up for work with a baseball glove. Playing baseball is
their job. About 750 of them
are major leaguers. Each plays
for an American League or
National League team. The
rest play in the minor leagues,

In spring training, big leaguers prepare for the coming season.

where they dream of making it to the "big leagues" some day. Every one of these professionals has something in common with you. They began by throwing, catching, and hitting with friends and family. How did they become pros?

For most, it starts with tee-ball. When kids are ready for "real" pitching, they move up to Little League. Little League Baseball is played all over the world by boys and girls between the ages of 7 and 12. When players get older, they try out for high-school ball. The top players make the varsity. Those still working on the basics play on the junior varsity.

Tee-ball is for younger kids (above). Little League (middle) and high-school baseball (bottom) is for older kids and teenagers.

After high school, the best players sometimes face a difficult decision. Each June, major-league teams choose young players in a "draft." Most of these play-ers also are offered baseball **scholarships** from colleges. Is it better to start a pro career right away, or spend the next few years playing in college while getting a free education? It's a difficult choice.

The best reason to play baseball is for the fun of it.

Whatever a young player chooses, the chances of making it to the big leagues are slim. That's why you play baseball for the fun of it.

To Find Out More

Here are some additional resources to help you learn more about baseball:

 **Books**

Baseball America Almanac, Baseball America, annual.

Gardiner-White, Sarah. **Like Father, Like Son: Baseball's Major League Families.** Scholastic Books, 1993.

Johnson, Lloyd. **Baseball's Dream Teams: The Greatest Major League Players Decade by Decade.** Crescent Books, 1990.

Lyons, Jeffrey, and Douglas B. Lyons. **Out of Left Field.** Times Books, 1998.

Neft, David S.; Richard M. Cohen; and Michael L. Neft. **The Sports Encyclopedia: Baseball.** St. Martin's Griffin, annual.

Ritter, Lawrence S. **Leagues Apart: The Men and Times of the Negro Baseball Leagues.** Morrow Junior Books, 1995.

Sloate, Susan. **Hot Shots: Greats of the Game When They Were Kids**. Sports Illustrated for Kids Books, 1991.

Stewart, Mark. **Baseball: A History of the National Pastime.** Franklin Watts, 1998.

Organizations and Online Sites

Baseball Hall of Fame
*http://www.
baseballhalloffame.org*

Find out about the greatest players in baseball history. The "Games & Activities" section tests your knowledge of the sport.

Exploratorium's Science of Baseball
*http://www.exploratorium.
edu/baseball*

Fun site that explains why a baseball curves, how to hit a home run, and many other interesting things about the game.

Little League Baseball
http://www.littleleague.org

Learn everything there is to know about Little League Baseball, from the history of the Little League World Series to information on summer camps.

Minor League Baseball
*http://www.
minorleaguebaseball.com*

Offers comprehensive information on every player, team, and league in the minors.

USA Baseball
*http://www.usabaseball.
com*

Provides information on national teams from the United States that compete in international tournaments and the Olympics.

Important Words

alternate to switch back and forth

aluminum type of metal

barrel widest and thickest part of a bat

manager person who makes all the important decisions for a baseball team during a game

pastime sport or hobby that people enjoy

precision the quality of being very exact

professionals people who are so good at something that they are paid to do it

reflexes the parts of one's brain and body that allow one to respond quickly to something

scholarships money awarded to students to help pay for a college education

umpire official who rules on plays during the game

Index

Meet the Author

Mike Kennedy is a freelance sportswriter whose work has ranged from Super Bowl coverage to historical research and analysis. He has profiled athletes in virtually every sport, including Peyton Manning, Bernie Williams, and Allen Iverson. He is a graduate of Franklin & Marshall College in Lancaster, Pennsylvania.

Mike has contributed his expertise to other books for young people, such as *Auto Racing: A History of Fast Cars and Fearless Drivers*. He has authored four other sports True Books, including *Basketball* and *Football*.